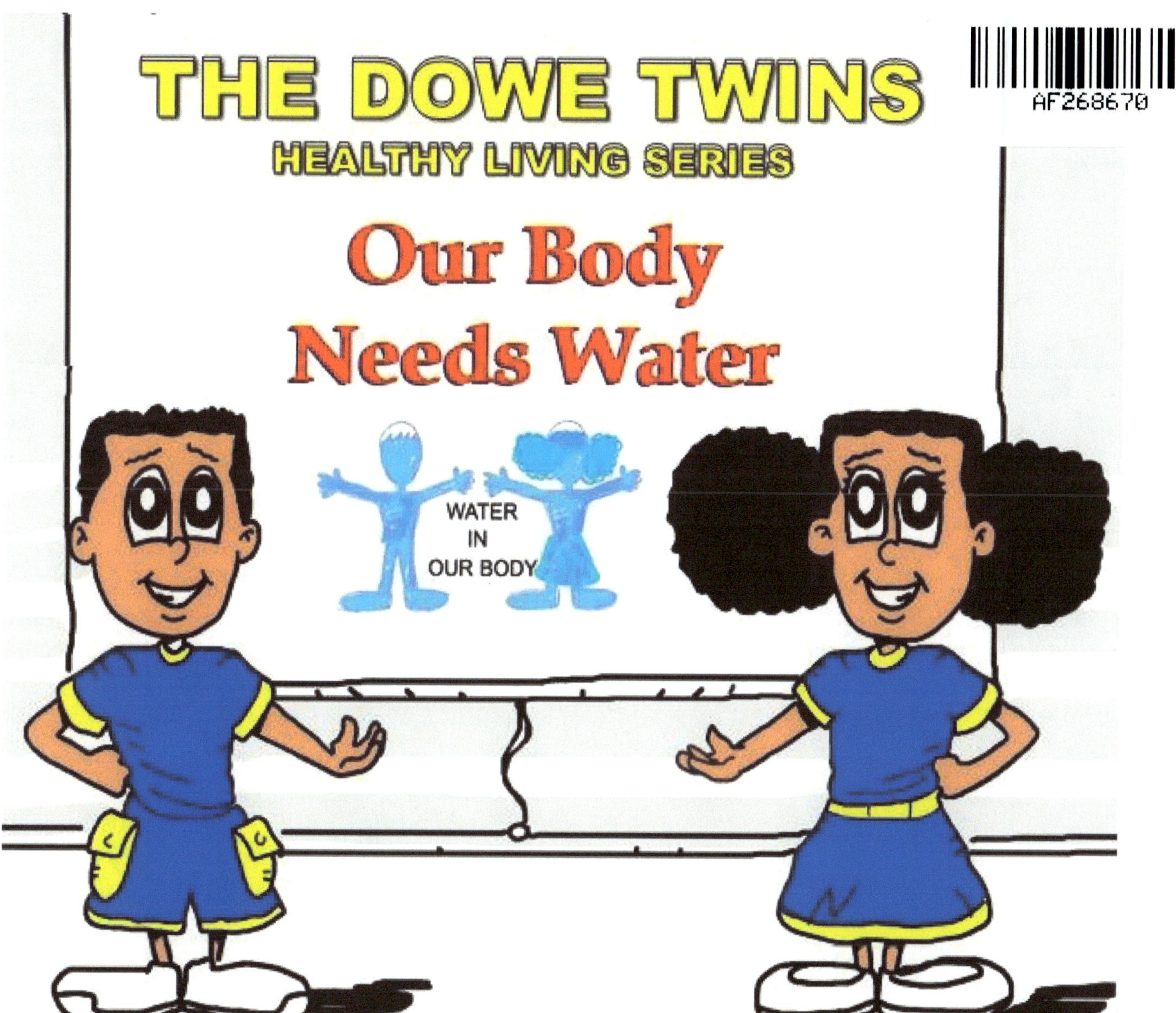

Adult Author: A.K. Dowe
Youth Authors: Princeton Dowe & Brazil Dowe
Illustrator: Bill Young

This Book Belongs To:

____

They just love meeting new friends. Every time they meet someone new they tell them who they are and what they do!

They work together every day to get kids "Hydrated, Healthy and Happy" the 3H Way!

They have an important health message they need to share!

They are only telling everyone because they care.

Just like plants, our body needs water
to survive.

Drinking water daily is a very important key
to being healthy, growing and staying alive.

Water does more than quench our thirst.

It keeps our body hydrated when we need it the most.

Drinking water when at play will keep
our body happy for the entire day.

Water works for our
body from head to toe.

Proper hydration helps our skin
keep its natural glow!

Drinking enough water can
even help our hair...

and nails to grow.

Water works to flush toxins from our body.

If we don't drink enough water we might not find it so easy to go potty.

Now we know water helps
our body in so many ways.

But our body also loses water every day.

While we are walking outside in the raining cold
or just enjoying the sun laying by the pool.

our body loses water more than we think.

When we don't drink enough water our body knows. It starts to feel sick and tired and moves slow.

Remember, like plants, our body needs water to survive.

Drinking water daily is a very important key to being healthy, growing and staying alive.

Now you have the Dowe Twins as your new friends and they hope you understand how important drinking water is...

so make sure to drink enough water daily, your body will say thank you later!

After Reading Exercise

How much water do you drink every day?

What will happen if plants don't get water?

What will happen if your body doesn't get water?

What is the first thing you should drink when you get up in the morning?

How many different ways do we use water?

Do you think this is an important message the Dowe Twins are telling you?

Can you think of other living things that drink water?

ABOUT THE AUTHORS

A.K. Dowe is an author on a mission to provide her twins with an understanding of the ways books are used to learn. Wanting to show her kids that books all have a different purpose, she started writing with them. She was able to show them that the words in books can be used to teach lessons or share someone's views. Starting with the intention only to help her kids, turned into The Dowe Twins children's book series. All of the books deliver a wide range of educational lessons in a fun way. With her mind set on uplifting and empowering the youth, she has also invited young artists to have an opportunity to share in bringing a few of the Dowe Twins stories alive. Providing them with a platform to highlight their artistic skills, with hopes to help youth artist build their portfolio and possibly start their career as an illustrator. All of the Dowe Twins books are inspired by the two kids we know as "The Dowe Twins."

Princeton and Brazil Dowe are brother and sister twins. These two are rambunctious youngsters; who enjoy swimming, soccer, and boxing. They are very active entrepreneurs and carry many professional titles. Yet their journey to writing started as a personal need to learn how to spell, read, and write sentences. Realizing that it doesn't come as naturally to everyone, they worked with their mom to create their own way of learning. Every day they continue to work towards mastering the foundation of early literacy. Using the experiences of their lives, one story at a time.

ABOUT THE ILLUSTRATOR

Bill Young is an amazing artist who discovered at an early age his love for drawing. He started out drawing ordinary objects and tracing images from comic books. As his artistic skills developed he knew his path to become a professional artist was irreversible. With an extraordinary passion for the arts, he finds joy in knowing he will be drawing forever.

To Our Readers,

We write to inspire, we write to educate, we write to show everyone that there are no limits to what you can do when you believe. To all the unique people in the world, we write to tell you never stop believing.

Thank you all for being you!

Sincerely,
A.K. Dowe & The Dowe Twins

Library of Congress Publication Data
A.K Dowe, Princeton Dowe and Brazil Dowe
The Dowe Twins Healthy Living Series, Our Body Needs Water
p.cm- (Healthy Living Series)
ISBN-13: 978-1644830000
ISBN-10: 1644830000

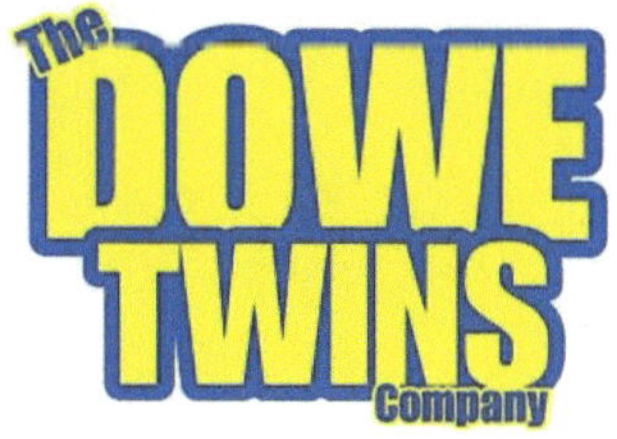

WANT TO BECOME AN AUTHOR?
WE OFFER SERVICES FROM CONCEPTION TO COMPLETION

GET STARTED TODAY
WITH PACKAGES FROM AS LITTLE AS $99

Just Call or Email

Ms. A. Kelly at 1(718)879-2717
alinakellypro@gmail.com

Be sure to check out
the other great books in
THE DOWE TWINS
book collection
www.DoweTwins.com

Also make sure be friends
with us on:
Facebook, Instagram & Twitter
@Dowe Twins

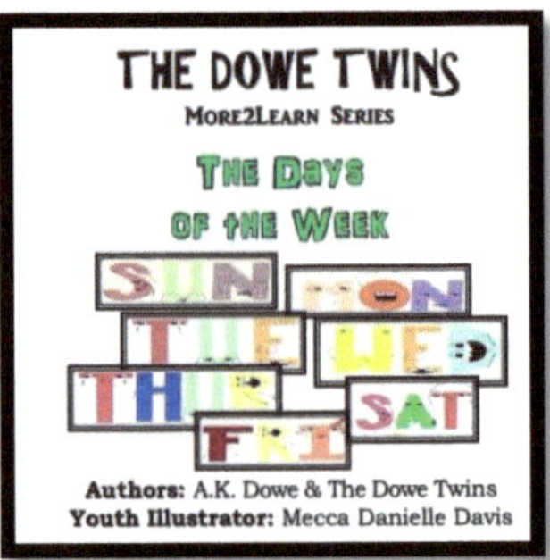

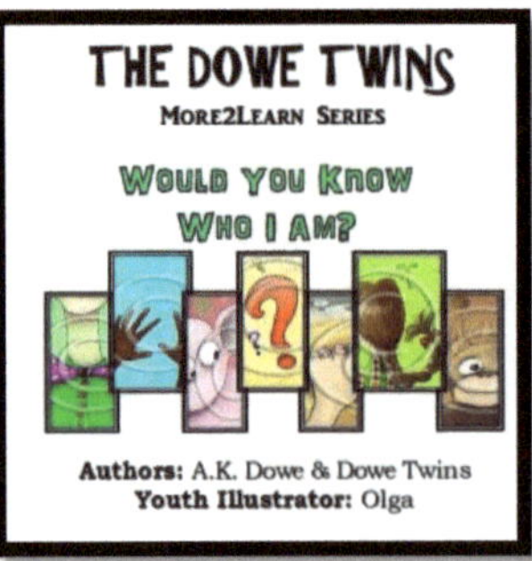

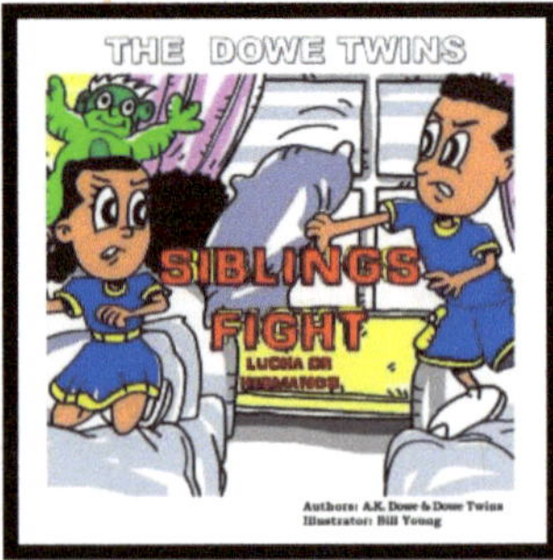

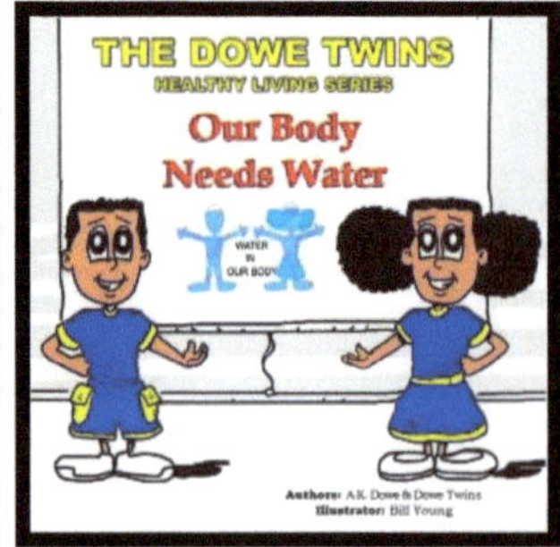